CONTENTS

San Francisco

 MANY PEOPLE MOVED to California during the Gold Rush of 1849. This new growth allowed California to become a state in 1850. People from all over the world immigrated to California. Many settled in San Francisco. The city was known as a place of "wealthy men and magnificent mansions." Beautiful hotels and dozens of businesses surrounded the center of the town. The Grand Opera House was popular and held many musical performances. Many famous musicians performed there. By 1906 San Francisco was a city bustling with culture.

▲ Market Street in 1899

▲ Photo of San Francisco in 1874

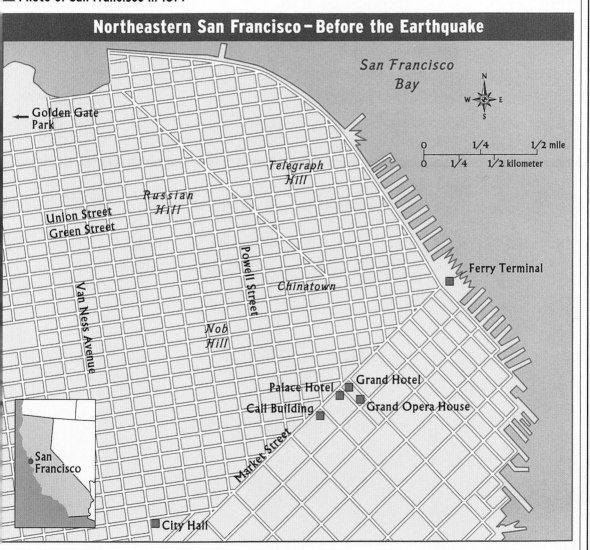

Northeastern San Francisco – Before the Earthquake

San Francisco Bay

Golden Gate Park

Telegraph Hill

Russian Hill

Union Street
Green Street

Powell Street

Chinatown

Van Ness Avenue

Nob Hill

Ferry Terminal

Palace Hotel
Call Building

Grand Hotel
Grand Opera House

San Francisco

Market Street

City Hall

THE SAN FRANCISCO
GRAND OPERA

PRESENTS

Appearing
!!APRIL 17!!
THE WORLD RENOWNED
TENOR ENRICO
CARUSO

SINGING IN
CARMEN
THE GEO. BIZET MASTERPIECE

SAN FRANCISCO

CHAPTER 1

Market Street

JACK COULTER STOOD motionless in front of the Grand Opera House as if he were glued to the sidewalk. People pushed past him on either side. Some of them glanced at the lanky boy wearing the wool cap that covered rust-colored hair. But Jack didn't seem to notice the people around him. He didn't notice the rumble of passing cable cars or the clickety-clack of horses' hooves on the streets. He just stared at the colorful posters flanking the Opera House's entrance. *Appearing April 17,* the posters read. *Enrico Caruso Singing in Carmen!*

Tonight, one of the most famous singers in the world would be performing right here in San Francisco. Jack was thrilled. Opera was certainly not Jack's favorite kind of music. He loved popular tunes, the kind people danced to. But Caruso had a voice like no one else. And that voice had made Caruso very rich and internationally known. A singer—that was what Jack wanted to be someday. Jack walked past the front of the theater and made his way around the back. He spotted the stage door. A wagon full of boxes stood next to it. As Jack watched, the door opened. Two men in coveralls stepped out. One of them shoved a piece of wood under the door, propping it open. Each man grabbed a box from the wagon and carried it inside the theater.

Curious, Jack approached the open door. He glanced around. No one was watching. What if Caruso were rehearsing inside the theater right now? Maybe he could catch a glimpse of the famous man. Or better yet, get his autograph! That would impress his friends—maybe even his father.

Without thinking what might happen if he got caught, Jack stepped through the doorway. It took a few seconds for his eyes to adjust to the dim light. All around him were piles of equipment and stage props. Extra chairs were stacked up against one wall. Jack slipped between two crates and tiptoed toward the dark velvet curtains that he guessed surrounded the stage. Beyond the curtains, people were talking. Very carefully, Jack parted the curtains a crack and peered out.

The stage was flooded with light. People were scurrying about, putting final touches on the scenery for the opera. A big man was barking out orders. At the front of the stage, a woman was setting up chairs for the musicians in the orchestra pit. Beyond that Jack could see rows and rows of plush seats on the main floor and in the balconies where the audience would sit.

There was no sign of Enrico Caruso. But just being near the stage made Jack tingle all over. How thrilling it would be to be out there in the spotlight, Jack thought, with the eyes of everyone in the audience fixed on him. Jack imagined himself on stage. Not Jack Coulter, the 12-year-old boy, but Jack Coulter, the world famous singer!

"Hey, kid!" an angry voice rasped out. "What are you doing in here?"

Jack whirled around. One of the men who had been unloading the truck was standing right behind him.

Jack swallowed hard. "Um … nothing, sir," Jack stammered, taking off his cap. "Just looking."

The man took a step toward Jack and peered down at him. Jack stared back, too scared to move.

The man bent down, until his face was just inches from Jack's. "Scram!"

The word unlocked Jack's muscles. He bolted past the man and ran. He didn't stop running until he was back on the street in front of the Opera House. Leaning against a lamppost, he stopped to catch his breath. A grin spread slowly across his face. What an adventure! He couldn't wait to tell Chin!

Chin! Jack reached for his pocket watch. His friend Chin Kwong was expecting him at three-thirty. Jack flipped open his watch. He was going to be late. It was already three-twenty. Getting to Chinatown would take at least fifteen minutes. Jack stuffed the watch back into his pocket and sprinted down the sidewalk. If he took the cable car down Market Street, though, he could save some time.

Of all the streets in San Francisco, Market Street was Jack's favorite. Market Street ran for three-and-a-half miles through the heart of the city—right down to the waterfront at the edge of San Francisco Bay. On this Tuesday afternoon, the street was alive with people and machines. Jack glanced down the street. A cable car was just screeching to a halt at the corner. Jack slipped nimbly through the crowd of people on the sidewalk. He jumped onto the cable car just as its bell clanged. The car jerked slightly and started moving, rumbling southwest.

Behind the trolley, at the eastern end of Market Street, Jack looked for the tall clock tower of the Ferry Terminal. Ferries came and went from there, carrying passengers back and forth across San Francisco Bay.

Jack paid his fare and moved up to the front of the car. Traffic was heavy. The wide street was choked with horse-drawn carriages and wagons. A few motorcars chugged along beside the cable car tracks, belching clouds of exhaust. People darted out among the moving vehicles. The noise of the street—men shouting, bells ringing, cable cars screeching, horns blowing, wheels rumbling along on the stone pavement—was music to Jack's ears.

Some of San Francisco's grandest buildings lined Market Street. City Hall was one of Jack's favorites. It was north of Market Street, surrounded by green lawns and topped by a magnificent, gleaming dome. He strained to see it, but he was too far away.

The cable car stopped. Several people jumped off. More got on. Then they were off again, moving past offices and fine shops, past the Grand Hotel and the huge Palace Hotel. The Palace was well named. It was six stories high and one of the most luxurious hotels in San Francisco. Jack had read in the paper that Caruso was staying there. When I'm a famous singer, he thought, maybe I'll stay there, too.

Moments later they passed the Call Building. It was San Francisco's tallest building, an astounding 315 feet high. Jack tilted his head back to see the top. It seemed as tall as a mountain, towering above the city.

When the cable car stopped at the next cross street, Jack hopped off. He hurried along the crowded sidewalk. It was choked with businessmen in dark suits, street vendors, ladies in fine dresses, deliverymen carrying packages, and newspaper boys shouting out the latest headlines. Above the din, Jack suddenly heard music. He stopped dead in his tracks. There was no mistaking that voice. It was Caruso.

Jack pushed his way through the crowd, following the music. It was coming from a large shop up ahead. The sign hanging over the storefront read "Bacigalupi's Music Emporium." In the window sat a brand new Edison phonograph. Beside it was a display of Caruso's latest recording, along with a poster advertising his appearance at the Opera House that night.

Jack stood outside the door of the music store, listening to the music, wanting to sing along. He was already late. A few minutes more wouldn't matter.

Inside the store, the music was much louder. Jack made his way up to the counter.

"That's Caruso singing, isn't it?" Jack asked the young man behind the counter.

The man smiled. "Yes. That's his latest record. It's been a best seller today, what with Caruso appearing at the Opera House and all. We've sold dozens of them."

"I'll take one, please," said Jack, pulling out his money. The clerk stepped away from the counter and came back with the record. Jack paid him and tucked the neatly wrapped record securely under his arm. He hadn't seen Caruso in person or gotten his autograph. But a record of the famous singer would do.

CHAPTER 2

Chinatown

BACK OUT ON MARKET STREET, Jack hurried to the corner and hopped on the cable car going up Powell Street. It would take him to Chinatown. The slant of the street quickly grew steeper and steeper. San Francisco was a city of hills. Three big hills—Russian Hill, Telegraph Hill, and Nob Hill—dominated this northeastern corner of the city. Powell Street ran close to Nob Hill. From his seat on the cable car, Jack could see the turrets and gables and slate roofs of the magnificent houses. Some of San Francisco's wealthiest citizens lived on Nob Hill in beautiful mansions.

Chinatown was a few blocks beyond and to the east of Nob Hill. The first Chinese immigrants had come to California after gold was discovered in the mid-1800s. They came by the thousands to work in the gold mines and on the railroads. Many settled in San Francisco, in the area between Nob Hill and Telegraph Hill that eventually came to be called Chinatown.

Jack had met Chin Kwong on his first trip to Chinatown the year before. Jack's older brother, Frank, had taken him there to see the Chinese New Year's celebration—the feast of the dragon, as the Chinese called it. The narrow streets had been packed. Red paper lanterns hung from balconies and storefronts. People were dressed in brightly colored silk clothing. The crowd had slowly followed an enormous paper dragon, brought to life by a handful of young men hidden beneath it. The air was filled with the noise of firecrackers, drums, shouts, and Chinese music.

It was the music that had excited Jack the most. As the dragon passed close to where Jack and his brother were standing, he noticed Chin, a boy about his own age, walking with other musicians. Chin was playing an instrument Jack had never seen before—a *sheng*. The instrument was made up of seventeen bamboo pipes of different lengths arranged in two triangular shapes. Later that day, Jack had struck up a conversation about music with Chin. They had been close friends ever since.

The cable car slowed as the street grew even steeper. At the next corner, Jack jumped off and stepped into what seemed like another world. The streets were alive with people with jet black hair and oval eyes. Signs on storefronts were lettered in bold Chinese characters. The conversations around him were all in Chinese. Chin had

taught Jack a few words. But he couldn't understand very much of what he heard.

As Jack walked farther into Chinatown, the streets became narrower and more crowded. Street vendors cooked over small charcoal fires that sent tiny plumes of smoke into the air. Jack passed fruit and vegetable stands, laundries, tailor shops, and temples. On one street there was a huge market where people were selling live chickens, ducks, turtles, and fish. Tucked here and there among the shops were tiny restaurants. The odor of fried shrimp and hot noodles wafted out of the doorways. Strains of Chinese music floated on the air.

In Chin's neighborhood, the shops and houses were very small. Many were built of wood rather than brick or stone. They were so close together there was hardly any space between the buildings. Paper lanterns dangled from most of the houses and storefronts.

"Ah, Jack!" cried Chin's mother when she opened the door. She was a tiny woman, but she hugged Jack hard enough to make him gasp. Then she stepped back and looked him up and down carefully.

"You too skinny," she said in her broken English. "I fix that!" she added, smiling. Jack loved the way Mrs. Kwong's eyes crinkled up at the edges when she smiled. And she smiled nearly all the time. She was the kindest woman he had ever known.

Chin's father had died shortly after the family had moved to San Francisco. Chin had been a baby then. He was Mrs. Kwong's only child. She made a modest living making herbal medicines and teas and selling them at several of the local markets. Jack closed his eyes and inhaled deeply. Wonderful spicy scents filled the tiny woodframe house. He loved being here.

Chin appeared from behind a bamboo curtain, his sheng in his hands. He grinned at Jack. "You're late!" he said. "You don't want to make your teacher mad."

Jack laughed and gave his friend a gentle punch in the shoulder. Chin was teaching Jack how to play the sheng.

Chin was a good teacher. But Jack had quickly learned that the instrument was very hard to play.

Mrs. Kwong patted Jack on the back. "You go, have lesson. I make tea."

"I've got something to tell you," Jack told Chin as they retreated to Chin's tiny room. "And something to show you," he added, holding up the record.

"Lesson first," replied Chin, looking serious. "Then you can tell me about your latest adventure."

For half an hour Jack practiced on the sheng. Chin corrected his mistakes. Sometimes he sang the melody, helping Jack find the right notes. Chin was not as good a singer as Jack. But he was a master on the sheng!

There was a soft tap on the doorframe. Mrs. Kwong pushed through the bamboo curtain that covered the doorway and set a tray with steaming cups of tea on the floor beside them. Small dishes were crowded around the teacups, filled with spicy fried shrimp, egg rolls, and other foods that Jack had come to love. She smiled and said just one word as she left: "Eat!"

While the two boys ate, Jack told Chin about sneaking backstage at the Opera House. Then Jack pulled out his record to show Chin.

"Too bad we can't play it here," said Chin, admiring it. "Maybe I can hear it at your house sometime."

A frown darkened Jack's face. He ran his fingers lightly over the sheng that he still held in his lap. "Chin," he said, glancing over at his friend. "My father gets angry every time I come over here."

For a moment, Chin was silent. "Because I'm Chinese?" he finally asked. His voice sounded heavy and sad.

"No," replied Jack, quickly. "It's not that." Jack shook his head. "It's because he doesn't want me to have anything to do with music. Any kind of music. He says I'll waste my life becoming a singer."

Chin nodded sympathetically. "That's hard, my friend. I am lucky. My mother thinks being a musician is a very honorable profession." He paused for a moment, resting his chin on his hand. "Wasn't your mother a pianist?"

"Yes, she was," Jack replied. "But I don't remember her. She left when I was just a baby. Some people say I look like her. But not Father. He never talks about her."

Chin looked at his friend thoughtfully. "You have great talent, Jack. But I can see you have a hard decision ahead."

"Yeah, me too," Jack said with a sigh. "Please myself or please my father."

THE SUN WAS LOW in the western sky when Jack left Chin's house and headed for home. A gentle breeze was blowing, bringing with it the scent of the ocean. Jack lived with his father just a dozen blocks away, on Union Street along the south side of Russian Hill. But it was a world away, in many respects. Jack's father made a good living as a doctor. They lived in a fine brick house on a wide street. It was very different from Chinatown.

As the sun began to set, Jack climbed the steps to the porch that wrapped around the front of his house. He pushed open the big wooden front door with its beveled glass window.

"Hey, little brother!" came his brother's booming voice from the parlor.

Surprised, Jack bounded into the next room. "Frank!" he cried. His brother was standing by the fireplace. Jack ran up to him, laughing. "Caught any bank robbers lately?"

Frank ruffled Jack's hair with one huge hand. Burly and broad-shouldered, Frank was ten years older than Jack. He was a policeman. He lived along the waterfront in a small apartment that looked out over the Bay.

"Nah," replied Frank. "Nothing that exciting. Thought I'd stop by for dinner. And speaking of dinner—you're just in time, Jack," he added. "Father said if you didn't get here in ten minutes, we'd eat without you."

The sound of clattering pots came from the kitchen. Katie, the woman who came in to cook their evening meal, was hard at work. Jack laid his new record down on top of the piano and sat down on the stool in front of it. He played a few chords. The piano was a beautiful instrument. It had belonged to his mother. But when she'd left, she'd left the piano behind.

Jack turned at the sound of footsteps. His father stood in the doorway, dressed in a dark suit. He was staring at Jack and frowning.

"Let me guess," Dr. Andrew Coulter said coldly, as he looked hard at Jack. "You've been to Chinatown again. Is that right?"

"Hello, Father." Jack let his hands slip off the piano keys. "I was just visiting Chin," he said defensively.

For several seconds, his father just stood there. The clock on the mantel struck seven o'clock. "And your school work?" his father asked, with an edge to his voice.

"I'll do it after dinner," Jack replied. "Look, I was just ..."

Dr. Coulter cut his son off in mid-sentence. "Jack, how many times do we have to have this discussion? You are not going to waste your life with music! It's time you dropped this fanciful notion you have of becoming a famous singer."

"Fanciful notion!" Jack cried. "It's what I want to do, Father!" He leaped to his feet. "Why do you hate music so much?"

"I don't hate music!" his father shot back. "But no son of mine is going to be a musician—singer, pianist, or otherwise!" He clenched his jaw. "It's . . . it's . . ." he stammered, "simply no way to make a living!"

Jack snatched up his new recording. "Here's Enrico Caruso's latest record," Jack cried fiercely, holding it above his head. "The music store sold dozens of them

today. And tonight Caruso is singing at the Opera House. Do you know how much he's being paid for his performance tonight?"

Frank and his father just stared at Jack. They'd never seen him like this before.

"Well, I'll tell you. Thirteen hundred and fifty dollars!" Jack cried.

Frank whistled softly. That was more money than he made in a year.

Jack sighed. "I believe I could make it as a singer, Father," he said softly. "I can't understand why you're so against it."

Dr. Coulter said nothing.

Frank cleared his throat. "How about we all have some dinner?"

Jack turned to his brother. "Sorry, Frank. I'm not feeling much like dinner. I'll see you soon, OK?" Jack strode past his father and climbed the stairs to his room.

How can I convince Father how important music is to me? Jack thought, as he crawled into bed. *What on earth will it take?*

CHAPTER 3

Terror Before Dawn

JACK WOKE WITH A START. At first he thought he was having a nightmare. Something weird was happening, but it wasn't a dream. His bed was shaking and his bedroom seemed to be moving in several different directions at once. The glass in his bedroom window shattered. Something in the ceiling popped. All the while a terrible sound like the roar of a huge lion filled the air, growing louder and louder. Jack tried to sit up, but the bed was pitching and jerking too hard. All he could do was to lie there and hang on.

It's an earthquake! Jack realized, suddenly fully awake. He'd felt earthquakes before. But never one like this.

In the moonlight streaming through the window, Jack watched in horror as the walls of his room quivered and began to bulge. A mirror fell with a crash. A bookcase collapsed, sending books spinning across the floor. The bureau on the other side of the room suddenly lurched forward. It seemed to be walking toward him. Then Jack heard wood splintering. The bed tilted sharply. There was a loud grinding sound overhead. A zigzagging crack opened in the ceiling directly over the bed. Jack covered his head with his arms as chunks of plaster rained down on him.

Jack rolled off the bed. He tried to stand up, but he couldn't. The floor was swaying, jerking, and tilting. Then suddenly, above the growling roar, there was a new sound, like a giant's teeth chattering. Jack's eyes grew wide as he realized what the sound was. The bricks of the

house's outer walls and its tall chimney were clacking against each other as they were shaken apart. Jack went cold with fear. The whole house could collapse! He and his father needed to get out!

"Father! Father!" Jack screamed as he crawled toward the door of his room. Beneath his hands, floorboards began to buckle and snap. Jack reached the doorway. He grabbed the doorknob and pulled himself up. Jack tugged on the door. It didn't move. Terrified, Jack leaned back and pulled with all his might. The hinges screamed and the door scraped against the floor. It opened about twelve inches before it jammed hard and would move no more. But it was enough. Jack squeezed through the opening and fell out into the hall.

From downstairs came the sounds of glass breaking and furniture falling. Unable to stand on the heaving floor, Jack crawled toward his father's room. Just as he reached the door, his father came stumbling out.

"Downstairs, Jack!" his father cried, grabbing him by the arm and pulling him to his feet. "We've got to get out before something gives way!"

Together they staggered down the steps. Halfway down, Jack felt the entire staircase tilting. He gripped the banister, sure that in the next second he and his father would be falling through the air. Just as he thought they'd go over the edge, the stairs tilted back the other way.

Seconds later, Jack's bare feet touched carpet. They were in the entryway. Overhead the chandelier swayed back and forth as if it were blowing in a high wind. The floor was strewn with toppled furniture, broken lamps, and broken plaster. From the dining room came the sound of dishes shattering.

Dr. Coulter yanked the front door open. Jack moved to step out, but his father's strong grip stopped him. Only then did Jack see that the porch was gone, collapsed into a heap of planks five or six feet below them. Jack's father sat down on the threshold and hopped down to the ground. As he reached up to help Jack climb down, a noise like an explosion came from deep within the house.

"Come on, boy! Grab on to me!" shouted Dr. Coulter. "The bricks of the chimney are falling down into the house!"

The next thing Jack knew, he was standing on cobblestones. Cool air flowed over Jack's sweaty face. All along Union Street, frightened people were streaming out of their houses. The street itself was moving, sinking in some places and bulging up in others. Jack watched in horror as a house across the street began to sway as if doing some crazy dance. Then it slid off to one side, collapsing into a heap of bricks and timbers and plaster.

And then, as suddenly as it started, the shaking stopped. People who were running stopped dead in their tracks. Except for the cries of the injured, the neighborhood was eerily still.

Jack suddenly realized his feet were cold and wet. He looked down. Water was flowing down the gutter.

His father noticed the water, too. "I'll bet the water mains have ruptured," he murmured. Then he bent down and looked closely at Jack. "Are you hurt, son?"

"I'm fine, Father," Jack replied. "I'm just scared."

"Understandable," Dr. Coulter admitted. "But it seems to be over now."

Across the street, a man was scrambling over the ruins of the collapsed house. He called out a woman's name.

Jack's father stood up. He stared at the house where minutes ago he and Jack had been sleeping. The sky was brightening, so it was easier to see. The chimney was gone and the entire house was leaning slightly to one side over the collapsed porch. All of the windows were broken.

"Jack," he said urgently, "people will have been injured. I need to do what I can to help them. But we can't walk around barefoot and in our pajamas. We both need to get clothes and shoes out of the house. I need to get my medical bag and bandages."

The idea of going back inside the house made Jack's stomach turn over. But his father was right.

Cautiously, they climbed back into the house through the open front doorway. Jack's father went first, testing the buckled floor of the entryway with every step to make sure they would bear his weight. The floor boards creaked and shuddered. But they held.

When they reached the center of the room, Jack's father stopped. "I'll go upstairs," he said, "and grab some clothing for each of us—get my bag. You go into the kitchen. Gather up as much food as you can carry. If you feel the ground start trembling again, run for the door or jump out a window. Understand?"

Jack nodded. He knew that they needed to hurry, but he was almost too afraid to move. He watched his father slowly climb the stairs. Then he gathered his courage and tiptoed toward the kitchen.

Everything was in ruins. The kitchen floor was littered with broken china and glass. The icebox had overturned, spilling the big chunk of ice out onto the floor. It was beginning to melt, sending little rivers of water out across the floor.

Jack spotted Katie's slippers beside the door. She always wore them when she cooked. Jack slipped them on. They didn't fit, but they would protect his feet. Next he found a basket and began pawing through the rubble for food. He discovered a box of rice and three bruised apples. One cupboard still hung on the wall above the sink, although it looked like it was hanging by a thread. Jack eased open the cupboard door. Inside he found a tin of tea and a larger tin of cookies and several jars of peaches. He added these things to the basket.

Jack could hear his father walking above him on the second floor. Tiny showers of plaster dust fell from the ceiling every time his father took a step. From the path of the plaster dust, Jack knew his father was heading for the stairs.

Jack took one more look around the kitchen. Just as he turned to leave, the first **aftershock** hit.

The whole house moaned as the ground shook violently. Plaster rained down on Jack, enveloping him in a cloud of chalky dust. Gasping for breath, he headed for the door. Then from overhead came several cracks so loud they sounded like rifle shots. As Jack reached the doorway, the kitchen ceiling fell in.

The impact knocked Jack to his knees and sent the basket flying. Out of the corner of his eye, Jack saw his father staggering down the stairs. Dr. Coulter gripped his medical bag in one hand. In the other was a bundle of clothes tied up in a sheet.

---

aftershock – a minor shock following the main shock of an earthquake

"Jack!" his father screamed. "Run for the door! It's going to collapse!"

Jack felt as if he were moving in slow motion. All around him the walls were cracking, buckling, and twisting. He turned and ran for his life. At the front door, he spun around. His father was twenty feet behind him, sprinting across the entryway. Jack looked on in horror as the last bolt holding the big chandelier snapped. Two hundred pounds of glass and metal came **plummeting** down. Missing Jack's father by inches, the chandelier exploded as it hit the floor.

Jack glimpsed the medical bag and the bundle of clothes whiz past him through the doorway. Then he felt his father's arm around his waist, pulling him out and away.

---

plummeting – falling down sharply and abruptly

CHAPTER 4

City on Fire

JACK SAT ON THE CURB outside the ruins of the house, trying to take in the destruction all around him. Many houses and other buildings along Union Street were badly damaged. Like the Coulter house and the one across the street, some had collapsed entirely, leaving only a pile of rubble where a building had been. Some of the ruins were smoldering. The air was filled with smoke and dust that dimmed the brightness of the midmorning sun.

Several people were wandering aimlessly up and down the street, looking dazed and confused. A group of men were searching for survivors and carrying injured people to the big **makeshift** tent made out of blankets that had been set up across the street. A few women were picking carefully through piles of rubble, looking for food or things they could salvage.

---

makeshift – built for temporary use

Shivering, Jack pulled up the collar of his jacket. He looked at his bandaged hand. When the house collapsed, a sliver of glass from the falling chandelier had been driven into his hand. His father had pulled it out and bandaged the wound. It was throbbing now. But Jack knew a cut on the hand was insignificant. He could see people with worse injuries around him. What was happening in the rest of the city? Was Frank safe? And what about Chin and his mother?

From across the street, Dr. Coulter stepped out of the tent, wiping his hands on a piece of cloth. The front of his shirt was streaked with dirt and blood. "Jack! How's your hand?" he called.

Jack jumped up and hurried over to the tent. "It's fine. It doesn't hurt anymore."

Dr. Coulter examined his son's hand. The bandage was dry. The bleeding had stopped. "Good," he said quietly. "See if you can find a metal bucket or two—anything that will hold water. I need a lot more boiled water for dressing people's wounds."

As Jack turned to go, they both heard a shout. A man in a policeman's uniform was running toward them up the street.

"It's Frank!" Jack cried, sprinting toward his older brother. Frank gathered Jack up in his muscular arms and hugged him hard.

"Thank goodness!" said Dr. Coulter, striding up to his older son.

Frank stared at what was left of their house. He shook his head and quickly turned back to his brother and father. His expression was grave. "I'm fine. I had to make sure you two were all right. But I can't stay. The earthquake did terrible damage all across the city. They're saying hundreds of buildings have collapsed. City Hall is a shambles. Telegraph and telephone lines are down. Far worse, though, are the fires. Fires flared up in dozens of places almost immediately after the quake. All the firemen in San Francisco have been called out."

"The situation is so bad," Frank continued, "that the mayor and the commander of the Army, General Funston, are bringing all available troops on the West Coast to San Francisco to keep order in the city and help survivors. The police and the military have set up their headquarters

in the Hall of Justice in Portsmouth Square. That's where I'm headed now."

Jack clutched at the sleeve of his brother's uniform. "Frank, do you know anything about what's happened in Chinatown?"

Frank looked sympathetically at his brother. "I heard that Chinatown was devastated."

Jack felt suddenly sick to his stomach. In his mind's eye, he could see Chin and his mother waving goodbye to him yesterday in front of their tiny house. Had he lost his friends in the earthquake? Jack knew that somehow he had to get to Chinatown.

Jack turned to face his father. He knew his father would say no, but he had to ask.

"Father," Jack said earnestly. "I need to go to Chinatown. I need to find out if Chin and his mother are all right. If they are hurt or in trouble, I need to help them."

"It's out of the question, Jack," replied his father, curtly, shaking his head. "It's too dangerous."

But Jack wasn't ready to give up. "Frank's going in that direction. He's a policeman, so I'll be safe with him. The Hall of Justice is near Chinatown."

For a moment, Jack thought his brother was going to protest. But instead Frank put his arm around Jack's shoulders. "I'll look after him," Frank said simply.

"Unless you need him here, he may be able to help where I'm going."

Andrew Coulter stood silently, looking at his two sons. He studied the anxious look in Jack's eyes. "It's true, there are enough people helping me here," he said slowly. Then he nodded slightly. "All right. You can go." He gripped Jack's arm and looked him directly in the eye. "But only if you stay with your brother," he added sternly, "and do exactly what he says."

Minutes later, Jack and Frank were hurrying down Union Street. Jack almost had to run to keep up with his brother's huge strides. Everywhere Jack looked there was devastation. The damage from the earthquake was far worse than he'd imagined. Not a pane of glass remained in most windows. Buildings had collapsed. Tall brick chimneys had toppled over or plunged through roofs. In places, the sidewalk was heaved up so badly that they had to walk around it. Groups of people clustered together in the streets, either homeless or too frightened to go back inside their damaged houses.

The two brothers had traveled only four blocks when a wagon drawn by two coal black horses came thundering up behind them. A police captain was driving the horses. Two more policemen stood behind him in the wagon.

"What's your name, officer?" shouted the police captain, bringing the horses clattering to a stop.

"Coulter, sir!" answered Frank. "Reporting to Portsmouth Square, sir!"

"Well, I'm ordering you to come with us to Market Street." The captain pointed at Jack. "Whoever that boy is, leave him!"

"I can't do that, sir!" Frank shot back. "This boy is my brother!"

The police captain's eyes narrowed. Then he shrugged. There was no time to argue. "Just make sure he doesn't get in the way!"

Jack and Frank leaped into the wagon as the captain snapped the reins. The horses tossed their heads and they were off.

Nothing prepared Jack for the scene they encountered when they turned onto Market Street. Columns of thick black smoke were rising ahead of them, darkening the sky. Throngs of dazed and terrified men, women, and children surged up the street. There were hundreds, perhaps thousands, of them all heading west, away from the downtown area.

Some people dragged trunks. Others carried suitcases or pulled children's wagon's piled high with whatever belongings they were able to save. Jack saw one woman carrying an ironing board and a flatiron. Another woman clutched an empty parrot cage in one hand and a bundle of clothing in the other.

Motorcars and horse-drawn carriages were weaving their way through the mass of people in the street. Some were carrying the wounded. Their drivers shouted at people on the street to get out of the way. As one carriage passed close by, Jack caught a glimpse of injured people lying in the back, covered in blood.

Soldiers in dark uniforms stood on some of the street corners. They carried large rifles. From the serious looks on their faces, Jack didn't think they would hesitate to shoot anyone they saw stealing from damaged and abandoned shops.

The wagon veered suddenly as the police captain drove around a cable car that had been flipped over onto its side. All along the street, cable car tracks were twisted or heaved up out of the cobblestones. Jack spotted several dead horses that had been killed by falling debris.

Frank nudged Jack and pointed off to their left. Jack stared at what remained of City Hall. The elegant building had been the pride of the city. Now it was little more than a huge pile of rubble. The dome was still in place, held up by a framework of steel beams. It looked like an enormous birdcage towering above the ruins.

Suddenly the ground began to tremble again. Another aftershock! The horses reared. Jack gripped the edge of the wagon as the front wheels were lifted off the ground. People around them began screaming and running in different directions. Jack watched in horror as a storefront buckled and slid down onto the sidewalk, instantly burying a man who'd been hurrying past. On one side of the wagon, a crack appeared in the street. It began to widen, as if huge unseen hands were tearing the ground apart. Then the quaking abruptly stopped. For a few seconds all was quiet. Then people started to move again, hurrying to escape the nightmare of Market Street.

Up ahead, and off to the right, a boiling mass of black smoke rose high into the air. Jack heard a crackling roar above the noise of the crowd. His heart began to pound with excitement and fear as he realized they were approaching an enormous, raging fire. Jack guessed it must be somewhere near the Opera House. Only yesterday, he'd been there, dreaming about his future.

When they reached the next corner, the fire came into view. It was huge. It spanned more than a city block. Jack had never seen anything so terrifying. Enormous tongues of orange flame shot out of windows and curled around rooftops. The heat was so intense that the air seemed to ripple and shimmer in front of Jack's eyes. The fire looked alive as it leaped from building to building, devouring everything in its path.

A strange wind swirled around Jack, tugging at his clothes as if pulling him toward the flames. Jack realized that the fire was creating its own wind. As superheated air near the flames sped toward the sky, it created a pulling draft that sucked air in from ground level all around the base of the flames.

A dozen firemen were retreating in front of the blaze. A few gripped fire hoses. But the hoses were flat and lifeless on the ground. There's no water, Jack thought. Water mains must be broken here, too.

Another policeman ran up to the wagon and spoke frantically to the captain, gesturing at the wall of flame. Jack looked down Market Street. Smoke was pouring from the top of the Call Building. Flames were shooting out of the ground floor. Other buildings were on fire, too, all along the south side of the street. At the end of Market Street, where the Ferry Terminal building stood, Jack could see nothing but smoke.

The police captain whirled around to face the men in the back of the wagon. "We can't help here! Fires are spreading and there's no water to fight them with! We're going to get new orders!"

Eager to escape the heat and the flames, the horses strained against their harnesses as they headed north and east toward Portsmouth Square. When they reached it a few minutes later, it was swarming with police and soldiers. The Hall of Justice had been turned into headquarters for police and soldiers, and members of the City Council, including the Mayor.

Jack stood quietly beside his brother as Frank received his orders and learned the latest news. In addition to the fires they'd just seen south of Market Street, fires had also broken out in dozens of other places, including the waterfront, the base of Nob Hill, and Chinatown. The fires were spreading quickly. Because of broken water mains, nearly all the fire hydrants were dry.

That left only one weapon to stop the spread of the flames: dynamite. By blowing up buildings ahead of the flames, officials hoped to create fire breaks—open spaces too wide for the fire to jump.

Frank was assigned to one of the dynamite squads. He took off his police cap and wiped the sweat from his forehead. "I shouldn't have brought you down here, Jack," he said tensely. "I never imagined it would be this bad. Now you can't come with me. And going to Chinatown is no longer an option."

Jack started to protest, but Frank cut him off. "Don't argue with me, Jack." He gripped his brother's shoulders hard. "Go home, Jack. Promise me that you'll go home."

Jack bit his lower lip. He looked up at his brother, reading the worry in his face. "I promise I'll go home," he said quietly.

Frank nodded. "I'll see you later," he said, trying to smile. Then he turned and disappeared out the door.

Jack stood as if rooted to the ground. Police and soldiers milled around him. What was he going to do? He walked slowly out of the building and down to the street. From where he stood he was just a few blocks away from Chin's house.

I promised Frank I'd go home, Jack said to himself. *And I will. After I go to Chinatown.*

CHAPTER 5

The Search

CHINATOWN WAS ALMOST unrecognizable. The narrow streets were choked with rubble. Some were blocked completely, forcing Jack to turn back and try a different route. At every turn, he passed tangled heaps of debris that had once been houses or shops. He didn't want to think about how many people must have been trapped and injured or killed when the earthquake hit that morning.

Dozens of small fires had sprung up among the ruins. Jack skirted several larger fires that grew bigger and fiercer even as he watched. Few people roamed the streets. Those who did looked frightened or lost.

When Jack finally reached the Kwongs' neighborhood, his heart sank. The damage was terrible. The streets were full of rubble and black smoke from a nearby fire. Jack picked his way through the ruins, looking for his friend's house. At last he found it—or what was left of it. The house looked as if it had caved in. All that remained was a pile of collapsed walls and splintered beams. Here and there, he spotted familiar objects: the rug from the Kwong's living room, some broken china, and a smashed paper lantern.

Jack closed his eyes. It felt like there was a great pressure inside his chest, pressure that had to be released.

"CHIN!" Jack screamed out at the top of his lungs. "CHIN KWONG!"

His voice echoed along the silent street. And then Jack thought he heard something.

Was his mind playing tricks on him? Jack wasn't sure, so he shouted again, "CHIN KWONG!"

He listened, hardly daring to breathe. There was the sound again. It was very soft and muffled. Was it a voice? He moved closer to the pile of rubble that had been the Kwongs' house. He called out. The sound came again. Now he was sure. It was a voice. And it was coming from under the pile.

Jack dug into the rubble, pushing aside broken boards. Every few seconds he stopped and called out again. The reply seemed louder, more urgent! Jack's bandaged hand began to throb. But he kept pulling and digging and pushing. Finally he came to what looked like the top of a table. He pulled with all his might. As the piece of wood slid back, a hole opened up below him.

"Help!" a raspy voice called out. "Help us!"

Jack peered into the hole. The dirt-streaked faces of Chin and Mrs. Kwong looked up from the darkness. Their eyes were wide with fear.

Chin's eyes grew even wider as he recognized Jack. "Help us get out, Jack! But don't move that big beam! It's keeping everything else from falling in!"

Jack leaned forward. He grabbed Mrs. Kwong's hand and helped her climb out of the hole. Then he reached down and pulled Chin up into the light.

"Are you hurt?" Jack asked, looking at them closely.

Chin took a deep breath, filling his lungs with fresh air. "No, not hurt," he answered, as he stared in disbelief at the destruction around them. He turned back to Jack. "When the earthquake hit, the house just collapsed around us. If that beam hadn't fallen the way it did, we would have been instantly crushed." Chin paused. "But we were trapped and couldn't get out. The pile of rubble on top of us was too heavy to move. We've been calling out for hours," he said hoarsely. "We'd given up hope that anyone would find us."

Mrs. Kwong took Jack's hand. "How is it that you are here?" she whispered, smiling.

From off in the distance came a muffled boom as a dynamite charge exploded. That explosion was followed by another, and then another. Overhead, the sky was so thick with smoke that it dimmed the light of the sun.

"I'll tell you everything later," Jack replied. "Right now we need to get out of here."

Chin and his mother were both very tired. They walked slowly. The sun had set by the time they all neared the base of Russian Hill. But it wasn't dark. The sky overhead was lit with an eerie red-orange light. It was the glow from the flames consuming San Francisco, reflected in the smoke that hung over the entire city like a dark shadow.

As the streets grew steeper, they stopped to look back out over the city. They could see fires raging along the eastern waterfront. All of Chinatown was ablaze. Smoke still billowed up from fires north and south of Market Street and from Nob Hill directly south of them. A wind from the east was pushing all the fires slowly but steadily west. Jack began to wonder if the whole city would go up in flames.

When they reached Jack's neighborhood, they found people camping in the street and cooking over small fires in the gutters. Jack saw that his father's "hospital tent" was still there. Nearly a dozen people were sitting or lying on the ground outside the tent, waiting for treatment. As they walked up, Dr. Coulter pushed open the tent flap and stepped out into the night air. He looked utterly exhausted.

"Father!" Jack called out, running up and throwing his arms around his father. For a moment, Dr. Coulter stared at Jack as if he didn't recognize him. When he did, he looked relieved, confused, and angry all at the same time.

"Jack—where's Frank? Why isn't he with you? Is he all right? Where have you been?"

Jack stood back. "Frank's fine. He's helping dynamite the fires." He turned to Chin and his mother. "You've met Chin, Father. This is Mrs. Kwong."

Jack then went on to describe all that had happened that day. When he got to the part about going to Chinatown, Dr. Coulter interrupted angrily.

"You went to Chinatown on your own—against your brother's order?"

Before Jack could respond, Mrs. Kwong spoke up in a soft and still-hoarse voice. "Your son. He save us. Without him, we die."

CHAPTER 6

Walls of Flame

BAARRROOM! At the sound of the explosion, Jack sat up, instantly awake. For a moment he was confused. Was it another earthquake? *Baaarrrroom!* An even louder explosion echoed through the morning air. Then he realized the explosions were dynamite charges going off.

Jack wondered how long he'd slept. He guessed it was close to noon. He looked around and spotted Chin curled up in a blanket a few feet away, still sound asleep. They had both been so tired. Jack pushed back the coat he'd slept under and stood up. He recognized the coat. It was his father's.

Familiar voices came from the hospital tent. Jack pulled back the flap and stepped inside.

Eight people lay on blankets inside the tent. All but one or two were badly injured. Several had broken bones. Dr. Coulter and Mrs. Kwong were kneeling beside a man who was moaning softly. Dr. Coulter was taking the man's pulse while Mrs. Kwong laid a clean bandage over a deep cut on the side of the man's head.

Dr. Coulter looked up and saw Jack. He showed Mrs. Kwong how to finish applying the bandage. Then he came over to Jack and the two of them stepped outside.

"Your Mrs. Kwong makes a good nurse," his father said. "She's been an enormous help. I even managed to get a few hours sleep while she looked after these people last night."

Dr. Coulter was quiet for a moment. When he spoke, his voice was very low and serious. "From the sound of the explosions, Jack, I'd guess the fires are still raging. And I think they're getting closer."

Jack agreed. The sharp smell of things burning, of ash and cinders, was very strong. And the great clouds of smoke were thicker overhead.

"Two of these people have only minor injuries and can walk," Dr. Coulter explained, nodding toward the tent. "But the rest can't. If the fire is coming this way . . . well . . . we'll need to get them to a safer place."

"I want you and Chin to find a policeman or a soldier—someone who knows what's happening," said Dr. Coulter. "There must be temporary hospitals set up around the city. We need a horse and wagon to transport these people to one of those places."

Jack sensed the urgency in his father's voice. He went and woke Chin. Minutes later the two boys were hurrying west along Union Street, heading toward Van Ness Avenue. Van Ness was a wide thoroughfare that ran north and south from Market Street all the way to the Bay. Jack guessed there would be many people there—maybe, some of them could help.

The earthquake had done quite a lot of damage along Van Ness. But most of the buildings were still standing. There were hundreds of people milling about in the street, listening to the constant explosions. They watched the clouds of smoke billow up from the parts of the city that lay to the south and east. They did not know where to go. There was shock and fear on their faces.

Jack and Chin began asking people for news. In minutes they had pieced together the story.

Fires were still burning out of control in many parts of the city. Firemen were working frantically to battle the blazes, but there was very little water to douse the flames. Dynamite squads were moving ahead of the firemen, blowing up buildings to try to create firebreaks. But so far, the blasting was not working. The fires seemed unstoppable and were spreading terrifyingly fast.

During the night, the fires that Jack had seen along Market Street had spread north and west. Early that morning, the fire had reached Nob Hill. Many of the grand mansions had been dynamited before the fire reached them. But it had not helped. The great houses were burning now, as flames engulfed Nob Hill.

Another wall of flames was approaching the southern end of Van Ness Avenue. Firefighters feared that if it crossed the avenue, the whole western part of San Francisco would burn. To try to stop the fire at Van Ness, every available fireman, policeman, soldier, sailor, and National Guardsman had been brought in to evacuate people on Van Ness and dynamite all the buildings along its east side. In doing that, they hoped to create a firebreak wide enough that the flames could not cross.

Jack felt panic begin to stir inside him as he scanned the avenue. If Nob Hill was on fire, and the fire kept moving north, then Russian Hill—and the injured people on Union Street—were right in its path.

Suddenly Chin was shouting and pointing down the street. A small horse-drawn cart, driven by a soldier, was coming down the street toward them. Jack ran out, waving his arms. "Stop!" he shouted. "We need help!"

"Out of the way, boy!" shouted the soldier.

But Jack wasn't about to give up. He sprinted along beside the moving cart. "You've got to stop. We've got injured people who need to be moved!" he cried.

The soldier yanked back on the reins, bringing the horse to a halt. "Injured? Where? And how many?" he demanded.

Jack explained, gesturing toward Union Street. For a moment, he thought the soldier was going to drive on. But the young man surprised him. "All right. We'll take them to Golden Gate Park. Get up here and hang on!"

Jack and Chin leaped up beside the soldier. As the horse galloped toward Union Street, the soldier told them that nearly ten thousand refugees were crowded into Golden Gate Park. The army had set up tents and was distributing food and water. A field hospital had been set up there too. Rumor had it that other parks and open spaces in the city were also full of homeless people who had fled the destruction from the earthquake and were now fleeing the fires.

Relief flooded over Dr. Coulter's face when he saw the boys drive up. He shook the soldier's hand gratefully, and then began getting his injured patients ready to move.

There was one big problem. The cart was only big enough to take three people at a time. They would have to make more than one trip. They all helped to lift the first three patients into the cart. Dr. Coulter climbed up beside the soldier. "We'll be back as soon as we can!" he called to them as the cart sped off.

Jack helped Mrs. Kwong and Chin get the next three patients ready. When that was done, there was little to do but wait. Jack decided to take one last look at what was left of his house. He wandered over to the ruined house and poked around the edges of the rubble. Here and there he spotted familiar objects: part of the clock in the hall, a chair, and some of his father's medical books.

He was about to turn away when something caught his eye under a tangle of splintered boards. Curious, Jack pulled the boards away until he realized what he'd found: his mother's piano. As Jack poked around the badly damaged instrument, he saw a small, familiar object. It was the new Enrico Caruso record, still in its wrapper. It was covered with plaster dust, but otherwise unharmed. Jack blew the dust off the paper. Holding it made him feel better somehow.

It wasn't until the middle of the afternoon that Dr. Coulter and the soldier returned.

"The dynamiting is continuing along the eastern

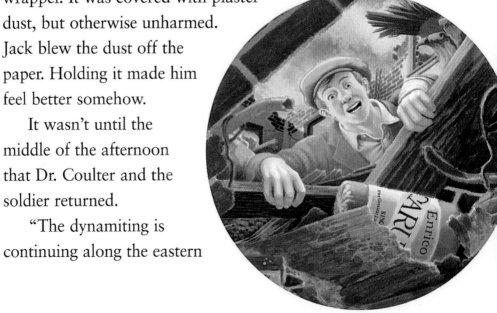

side of Van Ness Avenue," Dr. Coulter explained, as they lifted three more injured patients into the cart. "So far the fire hasn't jumped the avenue. That's the good news."

He paused to make sure the last patients were settled.

"The bad news," he said gesturing toward the south, where black smoke was boiling up into the sky, "is that the fires on Nob Hill are moving this way."

"Father, what should we do?" Jack asked.

"Be ready to run, all of you!" his father shouted back, climbing back up into the cart. "I'll be back as soon as I can. But if the fire gets here first, Jack, help the two patients who can walk and head for Van Ness!"

Before Jack could think to reply, his father was gone.

In the gathering darkness, Jack sat with Chin and his mother on the grass outside the tent. A blood-red glow hung over Nob Hill. As night fell, the glow turned darker and angrier. The smell of burning hung heavily in the air. Every few minutes, another explosion came from off in the direction of Van Ness Avenue.

Slowly but steadily, the fires to the south of Russian Hill edged closer and closer. By the time Dr. Coulter returned—long after midnight—they could see flames shooting up from the tops of buildings just a few blocks away. There was a sound, too, a dull roar. To Jack, the fire seemed like a huge, wild animal that growled as it ate its way toward them.

Dr. Coulter stared at the advancing fire. "So far the fire hasn't crossed Van Ness," he reported. "The fire break there seems to be working. But this fire," he muttered, "is getting too close for comfort. We have to leave . . . and quickly!"

Chin and Mrs. Kwong went to the tent and helped the last two injured people—two young women—get to their feet. Dr. Coulter grabbed his medical bag. Jack spotted his Caruso record, which he had left beside the tent. He picked it up and stuffed it inside his shirt.

They moved slowly down Union Street. In just minutes, the fire to their south had reached Green Street, just one block away. They could feel the heat from the flames now. Cinders and ash fell down on them like rain.

Jack looked up and watched the cinders swirling in the air above them. In the last few minutes, the wind had shifted. All day it had been blowing from the east, pushing the fires west in front of it. Now it was blowing in the opposite direction, from the west. *That's good,* Jack thought to himself. *The wind will help the firefighters. It will help keep the fire on the east side of Van Ness.*

"Just a few more blocks and we'll be on the avenue," said Dr. Coulter, encouragingly. The words were hardly out of his mouth when there was a tremendous explosion. It couldn't have been more than a block away. Jack watched in horror as huge chunks of burning wood sailed into the street right in front of them. More flaming debris crashed into the buildings on either side. Almost instantly, a huge wall of flame roared up in their path. The west wind fanned the flames. Now the flames were coming right toward them!

One of the young women screamed. "Hurry! This way!" urged Dr. Coulter, turning right up an alley. They were moving north now, parallel to Van Ness Avenue. "We need to run!" Dr. Coulter shouted. He picked up one of the young women in his arms. Jack and Chin each took a hand of the other women. Together they ran along the alley, dodging rubble, listening to the roar of the fire on their heels.

The alley led to another street. They turned left and kept running. Van Ness was just one block ahead.

When they reached the corner, they stopped, gasping for breath. The wide avenue in front of them was choked with people—thousands of people—moving as fast as they could to stay ahead of the advancing wall of flame.

Jack stared at the river of panicked people and back at the towering fire that grew nearer with each second. He realized the only way to escape being burned alive was to reach the Bay, and the water.

"Stay together!" Dr. Coulter shouted as he led them out into the streaming mass of people. Chin grabbed his mother's hand with his free one and they plunged into the crowd. People were screaming and crying, jostling to get ahead. *Don't trip!* Jack told himself. He knew, if he fell, he'd be trampled.

The agonizing escape from the fire seemed to go on and on. They passed street after street. The sky was brightening. It was nearly dawn. Finally, Jack glimpsed water far up ahead.

At the waterfront, people were packed onto the beaches and crowded onto the docks. Some leaped into the water. Other people pressed forward from behind. Behind them was nothing but flame and smoke.

But out in the Bay lay salvation. Dozens of boats and ships—all kinds and all sizes—were alongside the shore.

There were tugboats, Chinese junks, fishing boats, and rowboats. In the center of them all was a large Navy ship with the name USS *Chicago* lettered on its bow.

After a long while, Jack stepped down onto a worn wooden deck. He felt the sway of the ship as it left the burning shore and steamed across the Bay to safety.

THE TENT FLAP SNAPPED and fluttered in the breeze coming off the water. Jack stood beside it in the refugee camp, looking across the Bay to San Francisco. It was Sunday, April 22. San Francisco was in ruins. But it had not been completely destroyed. The day before, at 7:15 a.m., the Great Fire had been put out.

Jack finished his plate of food and looked back on the camp. The city of Oakland had welcomed thousands of refugees from the earthquake and fire. People were living in tents, waiting for the chance to return to San Francisco and begin rebuilding their houses, their businesses, and their lives.

News of Frank had reached them that morning. Jack's brother was exhausted but otherwise fine. He'd been one of the brave men who had kept the fire from crossing Van Ness Avenue and destroying the western half of the city.

Chin and his mother were fine, too. They had relatives in Oakland and were now living with them. Jack missed his friend—and his friend's smiling mother.

A few tents down from the one in which Jack and his father were living, a woman was unpacking a large trunk. Jack could hardly believe his eyes when she pulled out a **phonograph** machine and set it up on the ground. It still amazed him what people had saved from the fire. Jack thought for a moment. Then he slipped into the tent. He quickly found the record, still in its paper wrapper.

Jack walked over to the woman with the phonograph. He showed her the record. She nodded, smiling, and pointed to the machine. Jack unwrapped the record and slipped it onto the machine. He turned the crank and set the needle on the edge of the record. Enrico Caruso's

---

phonograph – record player

voice suddenly filled the air. All around, people turned to stare.

Jack just stood there, listening, enjoying the moment and the music. Then he felt a familiar hand on his shoulder.

Andrew Coulter stood beside his son and gazed out at San Francisco across the water. For a while, he just listened too.

"Strange how a disaster makes you realize what's really important in life," Jack's father said, finally. "There is going to be a lot of rebuilding in San Francisco in the coming months. But a city is more than just shops, houses, and hotels. It's also theater. And art. And music."

Surprised, Jack turned toward his father. Dr. Coulter went on, "We've been at odds, you and I, over music. You haven't understood why your love of music—and your talent—angered me so much. I don't think I really did either. Not until now."

"I loved your mother, Jack. When she left so suddenly, I was devastated. And very angry. Every time I watched you play the piano, or sing, you reminded me of her. So I took my anger out on you. That was very unfair."

Dr. Coulter looked down at his son. "If a musician is what you really want to be, Jack, that's fine. From now on, I'll help you instead of making your life harder, OK?"

Jack nodded. Then he closed his eyes and listened to the voice of Enrico Caruso drift out over the Bay.

The Great San Francisco Earthquake and Fire

▲ The Call Building and Market Street after the San Francisco earthquake

 AT 5:13 A.M. on April 18, 1906, residents of San Francisco, California, were awakened by a violent earthquake. The earthquake reached far beyond the city. The ground shifted and shook for more than 270 miles (435 kilometers) north and south of San Francisco.

The earthquake occurred along the San Andreas Fault. The land on one side of the fault moved about 21 feet (6.3 meters) past the land on the other side.

Understanding Earthquakes

In 1906, scientists didn't understand what faults are and why earthquakes occur along them. When the theory of plate tectonics was developed in the 1960s, this mystery was better understood.

Plate tectonics is a theory in geology that explains how Earth's crust is divided. The solid, rocky surface of our planet is made up of about 20 huge, stony slabs, known as tectonic plates. The plates fit together like the pieces of a jigsaw puzzle. But the plates also move very slowly. They float on a layer of molten rock called the mantle.

Faults occur where tectonic plates come together. These are not peaceful places. When plates collide, changes can occur on the surface of Earth. There are three ways that earthquakes can change Earth. If two plates continue to hit each other head-on, Earth's crust can slowly crumple up. This action causes mountain ranges to form.

Sometimes when the tectonic plates hit each other, one plate will slide beneath the other one. This can cause magma to build up between the plates. When the pressure of the magma builds up, the mountain can erupt as a volcano.

A third type of earthquake happens along a strike-slip fault. These earthquakes occur when tectonic plates collide and then slide past each other in opposite directions along the fault.

The force of an earthquake can affect people living along fault lines. Huge amounts of damage can be created when Earth's plates shift, including the breaking of water pipes and gas lines in cities near the fault line. Escaping gas can cause fires and broken water pipes can cause a shortage of water for fighting those fires.

The movement of the ground during an earthquake can cause buildings to shift. This could make them unsafe to live in or even cause them to collapse entirely. People can become injured or even lose their lives because of the fires or collapsing buildings.

▼ **People on Russian Hill watching the fire after the earthquake**

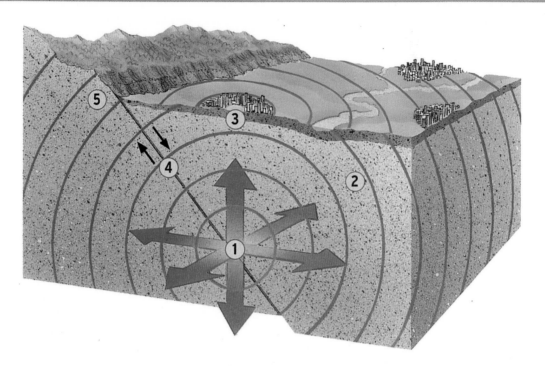

1. Two tectonic plates strike each other at the focus. This is where the earthquake begins.

2. The impact at the focus causes shock waves to move through Earth. These shock waves can cause buildings to collapse.

3. The epicenter is right above the focus. This is where the shock waves first reach Earth's surface.

4. The tectonic plates pass each other along the fault lines.

5. The movement of the tectonic plates causes Earth's crust to move.

Earthquake in San Francisco

The great San Francisco earthquake of 1906 was caused when the North American and Pacific Plates, suddenly slid past each other. It was one of the largest recorded earthquakes to hit North America. The first shock lasted about 45 seconds. It was followed by many aftershocks.

At that time, scientists measured the strength of earthquakes on the Rossi-Forel scale, which ran from 1 to 10. Ten was considered the strongest. The San Francisco earthquake was rated a 9. This would be less than 8 on the moment magnitude scale, which is used to measure the strength of earthquakes today.

The power of the earthquake brought about terrible destruction in San Francisco.

▲ The ruins of City Hall after the earthquake

in fighting the fire. It grew into a firestorm that threatened the entire city.

On Friday, April 20, more than 20,000 people were trapped at the north end of Van Ness Avenue. Under the direction of the crew of the USS *Chicago,* nearly all were rescued and carried to safety by boats and ships. The rescue became the largest evacuation of people by sea ever to take place in American waters. The fires were finally put out on April 21. The disaster claimed the lives of at least 3,000 people.

Recovery

After the San Francisco earthquake of 1906, recovery efforts began in full force. The army set to work keeping peace in the city.

Chimneys and smokestacks crumpled. Many storefronts slid into the streets. Streets buckled. Streetcar rails split and water mains ruptured. Entire buildings collapsed. Many people were killed when apartment buildings tumbled to the ground in a few seconds.

Fires started immediately. Walls of flame swept through the city. Towers of smoke from the fires could be seen far away. The earthquake caused most of the water mains to rupture beneath the streets. This meant that firefighters had almost no water to use

Many volunteers worked to distribute food and water, and to care for the injured.

Because so many houses and other buildings were destroyed, some people had to be moved to safer areas. Tents were set up as temporary housing for those who did not have anywhere to live. Various states raised money to help restore the city. New ideas were developed for rebuilding the city in a way that would reduce the dangers of fires during an earthquake.

Today there are new methods for constructing buildings that make them

▲ **Refugees waiting for food**

less likely to collapse during an earthquake. Water and gas lines are made out of more flexible materials. This means that they are designed to stay together even if they are pushed or pulled during an earthquake.

Today, scientists can help to predict earthquakes. They use special instruments to monitor movement in the ground. Scientists hope they will be able to warn people before an earthquake occurs. This will help decrease the number of people hurt by earthquakes.

We cannot stop the forces that change the surface of Earth. But people are working to lessen the destruction earthquakes cause. New construction

methods have made buildings safer. Scientists are finding ways to predict earthquakes. There is still a lot to learn about earthquakes. But today, people are safer than they were back in 1906.

▼ **San Francisco today**

Write an Eyewitness Account

THE SAN FRANCISCO EARTHQUAKE destroyed much of the city. It changed the lives of the people who lived there. There are many other earthquakes that have occurred throughout history and caused damage and destruction to the areas where tectonic plates meet.

- Choose an earthquake that has occurred in the past.

- Research the effects of the earthquake. What damage did it cause? What happened to the people who lived close to the earthquake?

- Write questions to guide your research. Then write the related information you find on note cards.

- Use the information you gather to write an eyewitness account of the earthquake. Write as if you were someone who witnessed the earthquake.

What did you do to prepare for the earthquake?

How did you feel during the earthquake?

What type of damage did the earthquake cause?

How did people recover from the earthquake?

Read More About Earthquakes

FIND AND READ more books about earthquakes. As you read, think about these questions. They will help you understand more about this topic.

- What are some causes of earthquakes?

- Can you name some of the major earthquakes in history?

- Can scientists predict when an earthquake is likely to happen? What instruments do they use?

- What are some of the ways people prepare for earthquakes?

- Why can earthquakes be dangerous?

SUGGESTED READING
Reading Expeditions
Earth Science:
Volcanoes and
Earthquakes

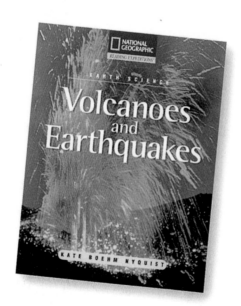